Antsy Ansel

ANSEL ADAMS, A LIFE IN NATURE

Cindy Jenson-Elliott

ILLUSTRATED BY *Christy Hale*

Christy Ottaviano Books

HENRY HOLT AND COMPANY

New York

Ansel was antsy.
He never walked—he ran.

When he sat, his feet danced.
Even his thoughts flew about like
a gull in a storm.
  Ansel noticed everything.
  And everyone noticed Ansel.
  "Pay attention," said his aunt.
  "Please sit still," begged his mother.

Sniff

SNAP!

CRASH!

"Why don't you go outside?"
suggested his father. So Ansel
did, whenever he could.

Ansel loved being outside. On the Golden Gate beach near his house, nature was big and loud and wild. Gusting gales pushed and pulled; salt spray stung his cheeks; surf pounded the sand—*BOOM!*

Sometimes nature SHOOK
with fury. In 1906, an earthquake
shiver-rumble-tumbled
San Francisco to the ground.

A temblor tossed four-year-old
Ansel into a brick wall, and he
broke his nose. Nature left its
mark on Ansel Adams.

But nature could be quiet, too. On Lobos Creek, it whispered and winked, flickered and flew, shimmered and shone for Ansel's eyes alone.

Indoors, Ansel felt trapped and sick. At school he got into trouble. Everyone thought they knew what he needed.

"Keep him calm," the doctor said, "away from light and sound." Ansel yearned for wind and waves.

"Give him discipline!" the principal said. Ansel felt like a fly buzzing inside a jar.

Ansel's father had a different idea. "Give him open air," he said. He took thirteen-year-old Ansel out of school and let him learn at home.

Piano lessons kept his hands busy
and his mind focused.

Between lessons in French, ancient Greek, and algebra, Ansel explored outdoors. He caught insects and made a museum in his dresser drawer. He scooped sand into cans and used a magnet to find flecks of iron. He gathered driftwood carved by the ocean, each piece a sculpture.

A season ticket to the San Francisco
world's fair filled Ansel's mind with
mysteries and marvels,
impressionists and organists,
flavors and aromas,
and fun and games.
Ansel was on fire for learning.

When Ansel was fourteen,
his aunt gave him a book about
Yosemite Valley. Ansel begged for
a visit. The trip took two days by
steam engine train and open-air bus.

At Valley View, Ansel got his first
glimpse of Yosemite Valley—the
ripple-rush-ROAR! of water
and light! Light! Light!

It was love at first sight.

One morning during the trip,
Ansel's parents gave him a camera.

He was off—

Run-leap-scramble—SNAP!

Rapid-rumble-
tumble—RACE!

Swoosh-
flutter-
flit—FLEE!

Ansel's photos became a
journal of everything he saw.

From then on, Ansel went to Yosemite,
camera in hand, to hike the High Sierra
   in summer light,
      icy white,
         glowing dawn,
            breathless height,
               danger by day,
                  sparkling night,
                     worlds of wonder—*snap!*—
                        in black and white.

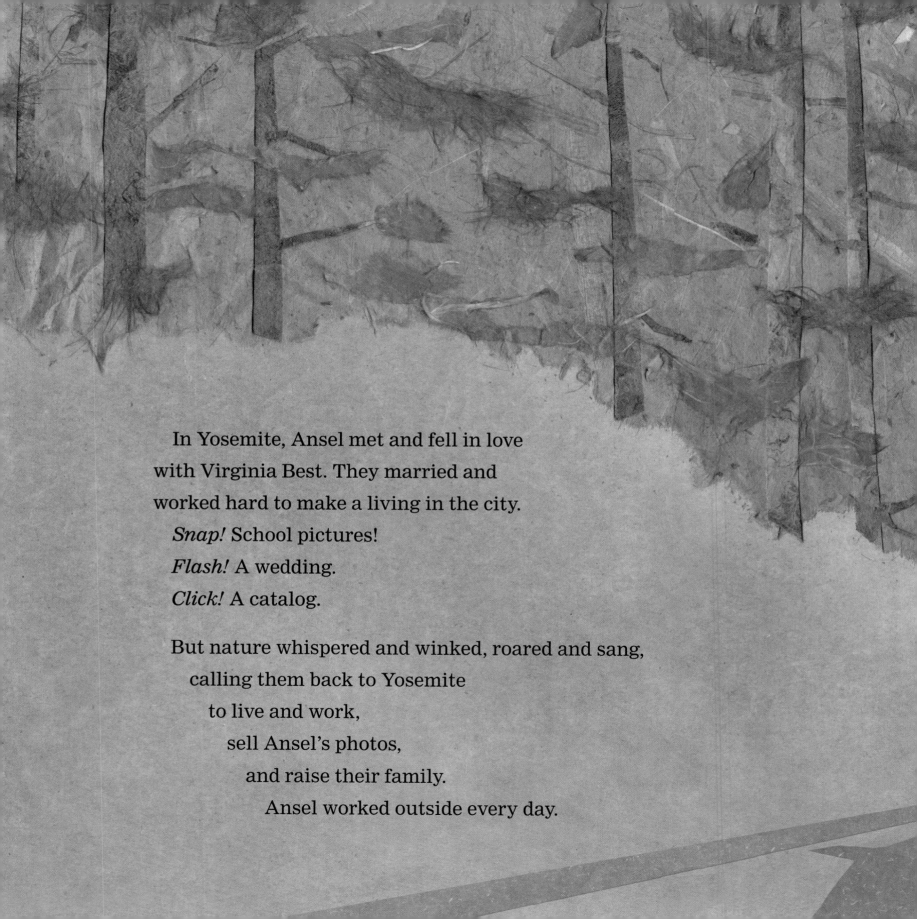

In Yosemite, Ansel met and fell in love
with Virginia Best. They married and
worked hard to make a living in the city.
  Snap! School pictures!
  Flash! A wedding.
  Click! A catalog.

But nature whispered and winked, roared and sang,
  calling them back to Yosemite
    to live and work,
      sell Ansel's photos,
        and raise their family.
          Ansel worked outside every day.

Soon, Ansel's photographs became famous.
When the United States government and
Life magazine asked him to take pictures,
Ansel traveled far and wide, showing
a nation its true nature in
national parks,
crystal caverns,
craggy peaks,
canyons carved by time,
silver rivers swirling
through wide-open land . . .

CARLSBAD CAVERNS

ROCKY MOUNTAIN NATIONAL PARK

GRAND CANYON

THE TETONS AND THE SNAKE RIVER

MESA VERDE

. . . giving voice to the voiceless and giving politics a purpose.

All his life, Ansel Adams noticed nature—
push-pull-flicker-wink-rush-roar-shimmer-shine!
Now everyone notices Ansel's pictures,
a world of wonder—*snap!*—
in light! Light! Light!

Ansel Adams: Life and Legacy

Ansel Adams was born on February 20, 1902, in San Francisco, California. By his own accounts, he was a nervous child, constantly talking, prone to illnesses, and unable to sit still or pay attention in school. In the early 1900s, few educators understood the needs of someone like Ansel Adams. Fortunately for him, his father did. Charles Hitchcock Adams understood his son's intelligence and his need to move. He provided him with access to nature.

In his autobiography, Ansel later wrote about his father:

> I often wonder at the strength and courage my father had in taking me out of the traditional school situation and providing me with these extraordinary learning experiences. . . . I trace who I am and the direction of my development to those years of growing up in our house on the dunes, propelled especially by an internal spark tenderly kept alive and glowing by my father.

The Adams family home was on the sand dunes near the Golden Gate, where the waters of San Francisco Bay meet the icy Pacific Ocean. There was no bridge back then, and Ansel had freedom and encouragement to explore nature—Lobos Creek, the Golden Gate dunes, cliffs, and Baker Beach.

When he was four years old, the great San Francisco earthquake struck the city, followed by tremendous fires that burned San Francisco to the ground. Since his family lived far from most other structures, the Adams home was spared. But the profound suffering he witnessed made a mark on him.

When he was thirteen, after some miserable years in schools that Adams later described as "grimly brown," his father hired a tutor and a piano instructor to teach Ansel at home. In 1915, his father bought him a season ticket to the Panama–Pacific International Exposition in San Francisco—the world's fair— and Ansel attended every day. Exploring art, hearing music, and observing inventions and cultures from all over the world opened Ansel's eyes to so many possibilities. The next year, the Adams family visited Yosemite for the first time, and Ansel received his first camera. All these experiences would prove crucial to his later development as an artist.

Much of the rest of Ansel Adams's life revolved around Yosemite. He was caretaker for the Sierra Club lodge in Yosemite Valley and led mule-train trips into the High Sierra. To capture pictures in the back country, Adams loaded 100 pounds of food and camera equipment onto the back of a burro. He stayed on the trail for weeks at a time.

Holding My Box Brownie Camera, Yosemite National Park, California, ca. 1918

When he was nineteen, Ansel met Virginia Best, an aspiring singer whose father owned Best's Studio in Yosemite Valley. They fell in love and, after a long on-again, off-again courtship, married in 1928. In 1930, struggling to decide between careers as a pianist or a photographer, Adams met photographer Paul Strand and artist Georgia O'Keeffe in New Mexico. They encouraged him to pursue fine art photography.

After the births of his children, Michael in 1933 and Anne in 1935, Adams turned to commercial photography to support his family in San Francisco. But he still found time to pursue his own vision of nature. In 1938, Ansel's photos of Kings Canyon in California helped convince President Franklin D. Roosevelt that it should become a national park. In 1941, the National Park Service commissioned Adams to take photos of national parks and monuments throughout the West.

Ansel Adams also contributed to many documentary photography projects for magazines such as *Life.* During World War II, Ansel Adams's photos of ordinary life in the Manzanar War Relocation Center influenced public opinion about the internment of Japanese Americans.

Ansel Adams's greatest impact was made in his photographs of nature. In 1980 he received the Presidential Medal of Freedom for his "efforts to preserve this country's wild and scenic areas, both in film and on Earth."

He died on Earth Day, April 22, 1984, in Monterey, California.

Clearing Winter Storm, Yosemite National Park, California, ca. 1937

Leaves, Mills College, California, ca. 1931

Photographic Visionary

Ansel Adams's most important contributions to the art of photography are evident in many of his pictures. Here are two examples of the thousands of photographs he created in his lifetime.

Clearing Winter Storm is an example of how Ansel Adams went to great lengths to show how grandiose nature could be. He ventured out in all kinds of weather to photograph the mountains, cliffs, and waterfalls and practiced what he called "visualization" in creating images. He would envision the final print before snapping the shutter, placing the camera in exactly the right spot to get the picture he imagined. This picture also shows his virtuosity in the darkroom, where he would use special tools to add light or shading onto an image in the process of developing a print.

Leaves, Mills College is an example of Ansel Adams's commitment to "straight" photography—photographs that depict the beauty of ordinary life as it is, devoid of romantic lighting or forced poses. This picture shows his extraordinary attention to detail and appreciation of beauty in the smallest, most insignificant aspects of nature. Ansel printed this photograph as a three-panel, five-foot screen, which graced his Carmel living room. Even enlarged, each feathery stem in the photo is sharp and crisp.

Resources

Adams, Ansel, with Mary Street Alinder. *Ansel Adams: An Autobiography*. Boston: Little, Brown, 1985.

Alinder, Mary Street. *Ansel Adams: A Biography*. New York: Henry Holt, 1996.

Newhall, Nancy. *Ansel Adams: The Eloquent Light*. San Francisco: Sierra Club Books, 1963.

Spaulding, Jonathan. *Ansel Adams and the American Landscape: A Biography*. Berkeley: University of California Press, 1995.

Stillman, Andrea G. *Looking at Ansel Adams: The Photographs and the Man*. New York: Little, Brown, 2012.

American Experience, pbs.org/wgbh/amex/ansel

Ansel Adams Gallery, anseladams.com

National Archives, archives.gov/research/ansel-adams

National Park Service, nps.gov/yose/historyculture/ansel-adams.htm

Sierra Club, sierraclub.org/history/ansel-adams

To Bill Jenson, Chris Elliott, and fathers everywhere who lead their children outdoors and into nature —C. J-E.

For my critique group: Lisa Brown, Julie Downing, Susan Gal, Katherine Tillotson, and Ashley Wolff —C. H.

Henry Holt and Company, LLC
Publishers since 1866
175 Fifth Avenue, New York, New York 10010
mackids.com

Henry Holt® is a registered trademark of Henry Holt and Company, LLC.
Text copyright © 2016 by Cindy Jenson-Elliott
Illustrations copyright © 2016 by Christy Hale
All rights reserved.

Images on pages 30–31 courtesy of the Center for Creative Photography,
University of Arizona © 2014 The Ansel Adams Publishing Rights Trust.

Library of Congress Cataloging-in-Publication Data
Jenson-Elliott, Cynthia L., author.
  Antsy Ansel : Ansel Adams, a life in nature / Cindy Jenson-Elliott ; illustrated by Christy Hale. — First edition.
     pages   cm
  Audience: Ages 5–9.
  Includes bibliographical references.
  ISBN 978-1-62779-082-6 (hardcover)
 1. Adams, Ansel, 1902–1984—Juvenile literature. 2. Photographers—United States—Biography—Juvenile literature.
 I. Hale, Christy, illustrator. II. Title.
  TR140.A3J46 2016   770.92—dc23   2015030944

Our books may be purchased in bulk for promotional, educational, or business use. Please contact your local
bookseller or the Macmillan Corporate and Premium Sales Department at (800) 221-7945 ext. 5442 or by e-mail at
MacmillanSpecialMarkets@macmillan.com.

First Edition—2016 / Book design by Christy Hale
The art was created by mixing traditional and digital collage techniques.
Printed in China by RR Donnelley Asia Printing Solutions Ltd., Dongguan City, Guangdong Province

10 9 8 7 6 5 4 3 2 1